AF269583

BOUNDARY TERRITORY

"*Boundary Territory* moves gracefully across species, geographical, and consciousness boundaries. Clever, funny, moving, and urgent, these poems experiment with form and content are wildly successful at invoking believable, sensory encounters between human and environment. I recommend these poems to readers interested in ecological relationality, interspecies communication, and the beautiful moments of being human in wild and not-so-wild places."

~Norah Bowman, author of *Breath, Like Water: An Anticolonial Romance*

Boundary Territory

Poems

Renée Harper

Copyright © 2024 by Renée Harper

All rights reserved. No part of this book may be used or reproduced
in any manner whatsoever without the prior written permission of the publisher,
except in the case of brief quotations embodied in reviews.

*Publisher's note: This book is a work of fiction. Names, characters, places and incidents
are either the product of the author's imagination or are used fictitiously, and any
resemblance to actual persons living or dead is entirely coincidental.*

Library and Archives Canada Cataloguing in Publication

Title: Boundary territory : poems / Renée Harper.

Names: Harper, Renée, (Professor of literature and creative writing), author.

Description: Includes index.

Identifiers: Canadiana 20240382714 | ISBN 9781989689776 (softcover)

Subjects: LCGFT: Poetry.

Classification: LCC PS8615.A7459 B68 2024 | DDC C811/.6—dc23

Printed and bound in Canada on 100% recycled paper.

Now Or Never Publishing
901, 163 Street
Surrey, British Columbia
Canada V4A 9T8

nonpublishing.com
Fighting Words.

We gratefully acknowledge the support of the Canada Council for the Arts
and the British Columbia Arts Council for our publishing program.

For Tyler and Elliot, who are my home.

TABLE OF CONTENTS

Boundary Territory

Geographic Coordinates

We are rooted–angular
within concrete assemblage
where roads denote use
while our homeless
teenage bodies twitch
against coordinates

The grid is rigid
        but we sidle
        its back alleys
working to undermine
        its patterns of use
                seeking the subordinate currents
and following the sylvan paths
        trod by hesitant predators and prey
at the small town's margins

Still, the valley is determinant
as every road runs some place
where someone extracts
use from resource
there is no wandering
        off these grids
but we try
        our worn shoes will find a way

A Coastline

When the freshwater lake
curls around your calves
follow her
the girl you were
to where she stands
in a baggy swimsuit
her tangled hair
face grim under
the coast's mute sun
watch her swim out too far
tease out currents with her toes
imagining she's some Ophelia
in a swirl of seaweed

Follow her
who smells of salt and dirt
who carves up the driveway
through blackberry vines
to the old house that sags
into the rainforest
heavy with ghosts

Follow her
through the weeds
into the kitchen
past the cold wood stove
up the painted stairs
to her attic room
with its small window
the twisted apple tree below
where in fall the raccoons
wail drunk on fruit and night

Sit with her now
on the narrow bed
in the lavender room
with her books and dolls
and watch her write in her diary:

These days become a murmur
they vanish   they fade
but still the currents carve
the coast line

A River

Land here where we watch daytime tv in a rundown motel room paid for by social services in a town where everything smells of cigarettes, borscht and the river that here forks and splits into fingers and tongues moving down valleys the waters maybe finding each other again one day in the Pacific or as cloud or maybe there is only dissipation and for now the river is frozen along its banks where the ice gathers and sings in the shallows where we tried to sleep under a bridge where it was dry and away from wind but the river rolled too near the ice jostling and the waters divorcing themselves from themselves so we walked on sore feet down the backroads and across the highway and the snow fell and our clothes were damp so we stood under the motel sign that almost felt warm as it bled orange light onto the snow and we watched and listened as the logging trucks rolled by

Trauma + Cigarettes

I don't know where we are but the valley widens and flattens and the farmland spreads to the blue hills and there's snow on the ground and stubborn tufts of yellow grass pierce the white of the low grey sky and the truck bounces over rough grade and we all smoke and I've gotten good at smoking do it like a cowboy in an old film squint-eyed and staring hard into nothing and the stranger talks and I don't like him but the place we're looking for is just up ahead and now it's always just up ahead

BALSAMROOT

Walk up the green hill
in worn skate shoes
feeling every rock
as you pass
bursts of balsamroot
their thick green leaves
their sunshine yellow flowers

move through them
with the mushrooms
you took in town
a faint static in your blood
Patsy Cline's *I Fall to Pieces*
in your fingertips
remembering that she fell
from a blue sky and landed
in a field a flowers

walk slow and further
up the hill and follow
your friend who
pulls thumb sized cacti
from the ratty hem
of her jeans

sit next to her
and pluck a flower
from its nest of green
pull its petals one by one
and make wishes for things
you can barely imagine:

a way past the valley
the town whose alleys
you walk where
you skip school
and bum smokes
and wait for a place
to crash

pluck the petals
and hum your song
the valley below you
the sky blue
the sun in pieces
falling from your fingers

Vanishing Point

She stands out front of Tastee Freez smoking a menthol cigarette. The evening rises around her. The dry pine covered hills are just there purple under a pink sky as she blows minty smoke towards the slow flow of small town traffic. Her heavy bag sits at her feet, a sturdy military sack packed tight as a sausage. Some men shout something at her from a passing car. She can't make out what they've said but curls inward as the bus finds the curb. She drops her cigarette in the gutter and pulls her heavy bags from the concrete. Finding her ticket, she boards. The bus is empty save for an elderly man who looks through dirty glass. She takes a seat in the back. Out the window, she disappears

Greyhound North

She longs for the clarity
of disaster on this
Greyhound bus
that travels north
of Clearwater pulsing
up the Yellowhead

Longs for the wildfires
that crest pine ridges
that find the highways
and devour the valleys

Longs for their flames
that leave nothing
but ash for the wide river
that might carry
the detritus of this place
to the hungry western sea

Star Children

Almost invisible under cedar / bodies pressed into roots and needles / the cold and damp of it working into second hand sweaters and worn jeans / they could leave, but they want to feel the transcendence that the pale hippy kid / his eyes thick with starry infinity / promised from under his dirty hair as he pressed the mycelium into their palms and whispered—travel far, star children / so they lay now under overgrowth / another accumulation to be absorbed by rain and slugs / all nutrients now / nothing cosmic here / just bodies cycling into soil / eager for the devouring

Luminous

Under the florescent lights of a bank machine vestibule / your winter skin green your coal hair blue / we are crowded for warmth under a sleeping bag away from the glass doors / outside wet snow falls in flakes the size of your palms / lands hard on the empty streets in this mill town in November / its close-knit community tucked under hand stitched quilts / you are here / pale but luminous / against the dark of this night

DECEMBER

A playground at dusk in mid-December no snow yet and you pull your jacket around your teenage body and look in the school windows where traced hands in fall colours are in static flight and there is nowhere to go but back to the crowded motel room but you are no female no human no animal no lightsome deer or soft-furred raccoon you are not a small plain bird capable of migration you will not go unnoticed with your face that radiates things you have no words for so you stay here in the playground waiting for leaves to take flight

Rainbows

A unicorn, a waterfall, mist and rainbows
an image that rests under heavy varnish
mounted on polished wood in a room
that smells of weed and cigarettes
of the bright birds who twitch
and chatter in a cage in the corner
the stranger presses weed and soft tobacco
into a rolling paper and twists
a story of a party gone wrong
silly girls eating poison mushrooms
wandering off and dying in the woods

And you listen and watch the unicorn
and when you tilt your head
rainbows fill the room

Abject

The rusted Pontiac follows them as they navigate the slush and snowbanks that line this stretch of rural highway where the sky is thick with valley cloud that rest heavy on the blue hills and his stepfather hangs his head out of the side window shouting about debts owed but she has nothing and neither does he and the snow is wet and her boots and pants are covered in road salt and mud and she ran out of clean clothes weeks ago and for weeks she can't stop crying, not dramatic soap opera sobbing but a slow steady kind that narrows her vision and softens the landscape and muffles his words while her hood is pulled over her ears her eyes on the road and when the yelling stops and the car pulls away to the wet highway throwing gravel and slush as it goes they will keep walking east towards the town the snow accumulating her boots wet and her feet heavy and years later she'll learn the word 'abject' and think of this.

Dust and Sunshine

An old car on a hot day
dust filters through sun
through open windows
they drove this road to that cabin
in this valley that felt like a secret
where night arrived heavy and dark
where that place became something forgotten
became half-remembered stale sheets
became faded floral curtains
became a self no longer herself
looking for a way back
to this same road
to dust and sunshine

Insomnia

You hunt indigo
at dusk on dirt roads
where you are barely human
the sky bleeding purple
into the old car where you sit
in the back passenger seat
and watch stars appear
in an inky firmament
feeling the curvature
of the earth beneath
the too big clothes
you've learned to wear

You're a plain bird now
nocturnal and hunting
in dark branches
rarely sleeping
or waking late with
the broken blue of dusk
shimmering around
your blackened eyes

ANOTHER ADOLESCENCE

Red jelly bracelets
on your teenage wrists
whisper hard rock candy rebellion
beneath an imagined
Ferris wheel with
a boy named Corey
who pouts with cherry tinted lips
under moussed blond locks
hands thrust deep
into acid wash pockets.

Half-drunk again
on bootlegged Lucky
Corey's words hum
with the orgasmic roar
of the big rides
while hornets buzz
around your caramel
dipped apple

And you want to rage
against the tame-town sunset
as you listen to Corey's Camaro
rev itself into a memory
off to find the back roads
with you intoxicated by
the smell of cotton candy
under summer stars

Chinook

It starts with a chinook blustering against dirty glass and the rocky
mountains distant again in the Whistle Stop but this time on a
Wednesday again in the red room with the low chairs the taxi-
dermy and the cheap draft that makes introductions easy over
green felt the low moon visible through the dirty windows over
the Colin range and it's breaking barren cloud as the day ebbs
into night and they blame the moon but it's the wind biting at
the cracks that urges townsfolk now drunk on a Wednesday into
unlikely unions urging them to plant seeds in this still frozen soil

Rotten Bones

Take the Yellowhead North
on a rain-soaked day
where low clouds cling
to too-steep mountains
watch for moose who
surface from swamps
antlers festooned in weeds
watch for wolves and deer
the *genius loci* of this nowhere place
who move from the undergrowth
speak another language
in their scutters and glides

as your old car pushes
through the Rockies
up the steep grades
listen to the engine
grind out its exhaustion
as your sip cold coffee
from a gas station cup
and mutter your verbal offerings
for passage from the spirits
but know they won't listen
to the likes of you

what with
your overflowing ashtray
your garbage strewn cockpit
your bad karma
from nights spent
in beds dank
with humiliations
inflicted or endured
on a back staff mattress
no, not with these
rotten bones restless
on this empty highway

So, flick your spent butt
out the cracked window
and concentrate harder
one day you'll get there

FUCK AROUND & FIND OUT

Find the meaning of life
at a punk rock show
at The Lucky circa '97
where you mosh in
in your army surplus pants
where your messy braids
whip against
the coming century

Frenetic in a mess
of anarchists + slackers
you thrash genderless
enraged at Enron + Bush
at the greed that renders
your lot ineffectual

And you fall into
a corner with your pal
pale faced with piercings
and eat her dry mushrooms
wash them down with warm beer
from a plastic cup smoke
a hand rolled cigarette
and watch the mosh pit
become sentient
nuclear-radiant in its fusion
of collective rage

'beautiful' you gasp
blow your smoke rings
into apathy—transcendent

Pancake Princess

Your hair dyed black
twisted into double buns
lips painted fire red
you were a pancake princess
who served skillets, shorts stacks
and recommendations for hikes
you'd never done

On your breaks
you smoked
by the grease trap
with the line cooks
who saved money to leave
but never left

You stayed too long too
through the quiet Octobers
the dark Novembers
the suicide months
of bodies in the black river
or hanging like ornaments
from pines on the ridges

You'd wait alone
for customers
that didn't come
wait for the drunks
on their way to the Stop
and follow them there
to drink draft
until you fell wild
a young elk on wobbly legs
in the empty streets
the wind from the glaciers
prying at your thin coat
your mascara running down
your painted face
your pancake crown askew

And you'd find your way back
to the empty staff house
to the mattress on the floor
to sleep and dream
of short stacks and skillets
nothing but this
and the mountains
you wouldn't climb

Hollow Ground

Stretched thin under high cumulous
the fields are an abdomen pulled tight

you like the animation of derricks
pulling oil from the plains

one day this province is going to collapse
so drive fast over this hollow ground

Adrift

a yellow cord explodes into tendrils
splays and drifts in the glassy water
behind in a small craft on a small lake
leaches in the mud a tent on the shore

he looks at you through tinted lenses
as dragonflies drone heavy-bodied
over the lake surface
and he dips a paddle into water
as you look north to the tree line
to the grey mountains
to the uncauterized cord
where you fray into air and water

Break Up

On a bluff above the frozen river
dry grass splinters below our tarps

we wait and watch and listen for
the sound of the river breaking

with the black birds that ride the currents
above our camp below the rockslide

shiny and slick they settle
in the sparse birch to acquire our diction

they have already mastered the sounds
of water dripping of children laughing of ice cracking
and are quick to mimic our squabbles

sunshine sometimes finds our faces
and laces our hair with gold and copper before
fading into cloud or night

and sometimes our words are warmer
and ease the feel of callused hands on softer skin

mostly we echo the frozen river and feel
for warmer currents that pry at older ice

Fool's Gold

Wash your face in the cold river
that flows to the Bering Sea
carrying the salt of you
to the salt of it

Stand in the sun that won't set
next to the mouth of a small creek
where you half-heartedly pan for gold
finding only tiny bits of pyrite
fool's gold that winks
from grains of sand

The man who will leave
your tent for another's
stands close by
his broad hat shadows
his face that frowns
at the creek
panned-out years ago

FORTUNES

Icebound above the frozen river
I met a man and we listened
for the river to break
the ice growing weak with
the strengthening sun
and in the dry grass
he read my fortune
in the passing clouds
ill omens mixed
with gusts of wind
but sunshine too
he said and left me
for the riverbanks
the wind blowing
across my palms

Weight and Gravity

Stand at the glacier's terminus / where ice ablates in milky streams / spilling sediments in rivulets that find their way to the rivers / you ascends the narrow path over fields of detritus and erratics / gape at the ice caverns / impossibly blue, impossibly cold / this place could kill you if you wanted it to

Broken Roots

Leave the place
slapped together in
a pioneer fever-dream
warped floors and crumpled news
that twitched from thin plaster
where the city blew through
the cracks with the smell
of the frozen lake and cigarettes
diesel fuel and dirty diapers

And arrive here
boxes stacked on neat
green grass surrounded
by too-blue mountains

Arrive a broken, breathing thing
a detritus
a bent frame
a mix of parts
a twist of broken roots

Between Catastrophes

In early April
clouds gather over
distant clearcut blocks
threatening wet snows or sudden deluge
the valley darkening beneath their mass
while the sun still shines here
on the bare earth fresh free of snow
still fallow with winter

Just so
you and I stand
between catastrophes
and the sun still shines on our faces
though clouds gather dark
over the clearcut blocks

SHIPWRECK

The house
is a shipwreck
in a temperate rainforest
all jutting ribs
and angry breaks
a secret catastrophe
a smothering
in moss and fern

Walk away now
your bare feet
on warm soil
a gentler tide waits.

Interior Valleys

(Re)Orchards: Work Shirts or Eden:

This paper is about orchards/blossoms
examines how work shirts become sites
where settler ambitions rest—nestled
goals are played out—how we turn text

to place: a failure where masculine and
Edenic narratives and the blossoms
reach-feel-house conclusions:

This paper is about dirt failure work
shirts wrestled in nested goals and
settlers making Edens in their own
dirty hollows—blossoms and played out
nestlings that settle in cuffs that house settlers
at/try reach conclusions:

This paper is about men masculine
blossoms and work bratwursts packed lunches
shirts discarded in orchards with conclusions
but more specifically nestled goals in dirt
and shirt sleeves sometimes work
often Edenic in nature or not:

This paper demonstrates that blossoms
sprout from hollows work shirts from
sites packed lunches bratwurst from
cool days from discarded narratives
or again nestled rested, the nestling is key
while settling remains dubious or so
the orchard suggests and the blossoms will show.

Nature Walk:

cold creek runs to the deep lake follow it over barbwire and cow
dung through muck and brush and needles and past condoms and
hippies camped out round twig fires high and higher on harder
and harder drugs past the angry woman in the pink track suit
with her mad little dog and past the old man with his metal
detector detecting but go undetected past the young guy on the
shiny bike who twists over broken ground all glee and Gore-Tex
past the naturalist who charts flora and fauna tilly hat on gray hair
past the young poet who hunts a muse in the water hunts a muse
in the dragonfly who here is ugly thick no magic on him past this
to the lake the shore the rocks the plastic bottle caps and faded
chip bags the squashed beer cans the abandoned fire pits the sticks
the rocks the sand the lake and into the water into the shallows
deeper deep down past the roar of jet skis and motorboats grow-
ing faint the water cold down to where the fish sleep big sleepy
fish green and grey with long whiskers brushing over algae
covered stones here we are what was it you wanted?

Find the Dark

Clouds catch on the bristle of beetle infected pine
over this valley that is slow consumed by stucco and asphalt
the sun sets over this and we hum to the blue lights
forget the beetles
forget the moon
except when it is full and presses
down on the valley
pries at the blinds urges
breast and bellies to swell
in rebellious remembrance of darker nights
and we go outside
find the dark
at the edge of the property line
listen to the insects in the branches
our homes hum electric behind us
the infected forests sing with night

Applied Theory

The dialogic chatter
of crows in the aspens
is a unification of ecologies
which is to say that
I can't help but run my fingers
over these bristles
this semiotic feathered skin

To put it another way
I ache for an integration
of my skin—bristling
with those ravens perched in the aspens
who explode into air currents
rise high enough to decenter this basin
(the dams, the roads, the concrete settlements)
and through their flight assume
an affirmative dissolution
of feathers
of hair
of roads
of dams
of settlements
of skin

Ravens who
sing / caw / enact
the animating tension
of this place
under the centrifuge
of these grey skies.

SMALL FLAMES

I don't collect stories
but use their scraps
to bolster a rib cage
a hollow shell
papier mâché in
my viscid hands

I don't collect stories
but swallow
the bitterest ones
with sweetened tea
feel them catch
in my windpipe
where they lodge
and nest like wasps

I don't collect stories
but weave them
into my silvering hair
fashioning a crown of tangles
poison vines in starlight

I don't collect stories
but burn them here
in this cold pit
their small flames
light up the dark

ANOTHER OKANAGAN

Under kerosene lamps & imperial bunting a man is dressed in the kind of thick red velvet used in funeral parlours / a pocket watch chain hangs limp from a waistcoat's brass button / but there is no watch to tick against the night / his hair hangs long & dry golden like the grasses that line the dirt road on the way out of town in mid-August / when the snakes sleep at noon but wake at dusk and rattle their way down to the cool waters of the painted lake / under kerosene lamps & imperial bunting he grins with thin lips / winks at her / his hands deep in his pockets while the band plays old songs from far away and across a sea / and inside the canvas tent the dancers sway with phantoms and she grins at this devil / a snake in the water / the night quiet over the dry hills

A WESTERN

In a valley that was home
where bodies are rumoured
buried in a neglected orchard

Walk past
the trees heavy
with overripe fruit
where the wasps drone
with hunger and menace

Walk fast
before the skies erupt
in bruised clouds
that heave lightning
at the blue hills

Leave before
the hills catch with fires
that sidle down ravines
that pour into town
over dry highways

Walk fast
before the old ghosts
wreathed in
cigarette smoke
in dirty jeans
arrive
riding full saddle
though our desolation
evacuation orders
on dry lips

Affirmations + Eco-Grief

Everything is fuel
for growth and connection

Especially the parched undergrowth
that crowds the forests floors
where flames start slow
but spiral into vortexes
their sparks catching
on westerly winds
their growth
exponential

Thoughts are passing clouds
and I am the sky

Full of dangerous particulates
an anxious concentration
of pollutants
full of my own
noxious insistence on
now impossible comforts

On Limping Foot

Snow decays
in the winter shadows
as controlled flames
devour slash piles
orange pyres on brown earth
their smoke spills like an omen
into the exhausted valley

I think of Greek tragedy
how punishments sometimes
comes on limping foot
pede poena claudo

How summer will arrive
slow then withering
these valleys erupting
in conflagrations
this ridge then that
water bombers in the orange skies
thrumming harpies
that sing a song of ruin

Long Winter

I.

Build a bunker
burrow in rocky soil
you are an owl now
with dirty feathers
a flexible neck that twists
this way and that
listening listening

II.

Ingest potassium iodide
and feel it saturate
your thyroid gland
the salt of it
will decay with you
into the poisoned sea

III.

Remove your clothing
contaminated by particulates
but do it slowly
don't reveal
too much too soon
leave some mystery
as you gyrate
in the lantern light
radiant—radiating

IV.

Finally, eat the peaches
you canned in August
let the juice of them
run down your chest
the long winter
is here at last

Water & Stone

Past midnight in late August
the valleys are acrid with wildfire
in the creek the salmon
are dying seasonal deaths

I can hear their fins
break on the smooth stones
see their eyes grow cloudy
as they slide
into the eddies
where the clear waters pool

I can hear them now
fins and scales
water and stone

We won't sleep tonight
fires burning to the south
the cold creek running still

FISSURES

Spend a morning parsing
the language of socio-spatial dialects
washed down with cold coffee
my brow collapsing into valleys
where I trace splinters
in the epistemic landscape
delineate furrows in the interstice
where I feel my failure
language silt and sand
and know only that these valleys
are not for my bones
culpable in the dynamics
of encroachment

Still, I live in the fissures
with this notebook this body
another irritant under
smoke filled skies.

The Orchard

Leave your old car in the ditch
and walk up the soft slope of
the mountain, snow to your knees
home is just past the abandoned farm
through the orchard where your
rented cabin waits with tea and blankets

Leave the road and
step into the snowy field
where the night quiets
and the only sound
is your laboured breath
your reliable heart
your muffled steps that
carry you through
this silent sweep

Move under low clouds
away from the streetlamp
that stands a mute vigil
over the rural crossroad
slide into more dark
flashlight in hand
and carve a flickering path
into the orchard abandoned
by its planters decades ago
where in late August
you harvested small fruit
dusty plums and yellow apples
mottled and sweet filling your basket
bees singing in the undergrowth

Now the night is humid
And you move under winter layers
shine your light in the grove
and find the snowy torsos
find the boughs the elegant limbs
the fingers that twist
into the night's obscured heavens

Crowsnest Hwy

words are dark rainbows:
that's what he wrote having wound down
this road too many mornings
fog and elk and blood
sometimes stopping
next to the damned river
pondering something indecent that happened
next to another river the logging trucks rolling past

I wind down this road and words unfurl about
unhappy crows that pick at a half-concealed carcass
disturbed and taking wing, but the tires grip the road
and those ravines aren't calling and sure maybe
out there the sodden ground urges on some
coming-darkness and sniffs out the weak—the slow
who fall on wet leaves that become palliative

but here, on this sinuous road
we sit, him and I, preening glossy feathers
dark words prismatic between us ever-rapturous
of these old margins, of the black birds that caw against
the shorter days and explode from ditches leaving
our sad mouthed carcasses
yawning at the grey

★ "What can be said? Words are dark rainbows." from Patrick Lane's poem,
"A Murder of Crows." Lane, Patrick. *The Collected Poems of Patrick Lane.*
Eds. Donna Bennett, and Russell Brown. Madeira Park, BC: Harbour
Publishing, 2011.

Ghost Image

Your old blue mustang
pries up the thin road
that twists through
the Eastern slopes
of the Northern Rockies
towards an abandoned
coal mine near Cadomin, Alberta

The river is in full flood
mountains are grey teeth
as your smoke fills the cab
your silver hair full
of early spring sun

So cool in your dark glasses
40 years my senior
I want to be you
the big city photographer
who landed
in these mountains
in winter who arrived
with flat boxes filled
with pictures
of ancient ruins
of muscled men posing
Adonises in junk yards
of thin women with red lips
in ludicrous hats angular
before city skylines

But my favourites
are your self-portraits
you in black and white
a punk in leather
a cigarette never far
from thin lips that curl
in a wolf's snarl

I'd follow you
anywhere
I follow you
up that road
to that ghost town
its abandoned mine
to take photographs
of crumbling infrastructure
of coal heaps and tailings ponds
of desolation the clouds gathering
heavy over the tired mountains
    your dark glasses
    hiding   your eyes
    hiding   your diagnosis

You don't tell me
    you won't make it
to summer instead
you take photos
on film   you won't develop
  leaving me with traces
       a ghost image of you

Extraction

This body instrumentalized
turbulent through turbines
howls under clear skies
in early spring

As the flood unearths bones
that swirl in eddies dislodged
from the banks

As mournful songs
rise from its body its currents
and gather in the pools where
the water slows

Still, this body sings
electric-reluctant but
aqueous and acquiescing
within a topography
run through systems designed
to store-manage-display-analyze
all types of geographic and spatial data

that render this place
these bones pliable
a *matériel* for extraction

Still, as it ever was,
this body moves south
its voice raw with the flood
over spillways its flow velocity
pounding against barrages
that will one day fail
or be dismantled

And I am small
by the side of the highway
my car still running
the radio drowned
by the steady roar
of water through turbines

materiel: "To make things into tools in the first place, we remove them from autonomous existence and conscript them as servants, determining their immediate futures."—McKay, Don. "Baler Twine: Thoughts on Ravens, Home, and Nature Poetry." *Studies in Canadian Literature / Études en littérature canadienne*, 18.1 (1993): n. pag.

Lines of Inquiry

Under heavy cloud in a thin valley
where a river runs south
before being damned
epistemic practices produce
habitats where bodies dwell
where geography is fate

But open palms invite
re-mappings
invite fingers to trace
paths of inquiry
through sylvan systems
where trees shed bright leaves
where cold feet on the damp earth
amounts to an invitation

The Fool

Fires burning to the south
smoke settling heavy
in the dry valley
she slides from the van
its dirty linens
in her festival finery
all magic in the high
yellow boots she bought
from the bazaar
all magic in her dead aunt's
floral tunic that smells
of long smoked cigarettes
of her sweat and joy
her aunt walks with her now
a long red feather pinned
in her silvering hair
as she moves through
the drought scarred field
pulls sour scented daisies
from the grasses as she moves
towards the music its
exhalations communicable
she joins them in her finery
they are birds drunk
on fermented berries
dizzy in the bush
the fires far
away for now

Ravine

Sockeyes rot next
to a cold creek
flesh and scales
and clouded eyes that don't see
your boots that leave
prints in the mud
stop on the eroding bank
to smoke and watch
the dead eyes watch the sky
through the branches
none of the usual predators
just boots and eyes and brush
just another intruder intruding
who gazes at a dead fish that rots
having spawned maybe successful
as the world collapses above the ravine

Here some of the dying is done
step heavy on the eroding banks
speed on the inevitable

Whichever Stone

Whichever stone you turn
there are microhabitats
for cylindrical bodies that coil
in the sun and ache
for the shadow of the stone
you hold in your hand
violence in your fingers
the day is still long

Oumuamua

They appear from
the direction of Vega
in the constellation of Lyra
unbothered they tumble interstellar
move 6° from the solar apex
their system of origin
and age unknown

Some hypothesize
they're here to observe
our inelegant self-immolation
so you look for them
in the night sky
sit in your camp chair
offer your embers to the stars

HYDROLOGY/SNAP PEAS

In addition to establishing a *modus operandum*
that listens to the movement of honeybees and
registers the faint trace of pollen on the hands of
my child in late spring, the sun in his copper hair
we work now (mother+son) to delineate the bioregion
to live in its crevices and observe the streams that make
plain stones into gems, that carve new lines into our palms
open even eager for the proactive force of geology for
the social and political forces inherent in sweet-snap-peas
lean, long and teeming with evolving dialogues of seasons
and silverware collections, of fading family photos unboxed
of land claims and atrocities in green trees of these migrations
(forced sometimes) that paused but never quite imbedded
in tough soil, but hydrological in character eroding all
so pause here in a garden with a child who snaps up
peas and exults in the polyphonic green of the
space that he dwells, pollen on busy fingertips
a means-of-being if only for now

West Wind & Wrack

I want to be beautiful
to be light piercing storm clouds

sharp light that becomes stark shafts
falling onto unsettled water

I want to be stark and unsettled
a shudder of west wind that raises swells

to be a shudder of rough waves on wet stones
a thing that leaves wrack in tortuous drifts

I want to be the wraith that churns water
that leaves wrack along a path at the water's edge

I want to be the wet stones at the water's edge
to be light piercing storm clouds
to be the waves that churn
to be the west wind
and the wrack

I want to be beautiful

Maybe Homelands

Omens

Unbend here
brokenly
under charred black branches
boughs a busted cage

Here we are
metaphors
ready vessels
who drink wine
from metal cups
next to a campfire
who can divine
fortunes
in the embers
read the stars
through the branches

brokenly—branch by branch
our omens are heavy in the boughs

Burning Windmill

A sweep of sails
on fire over
a brown canal
unthinkable orange
against delft blue night

an act of war
and the beginning
of me knowing you

Black Bird

Someone took a picture of the ruins
of my great grandfather's windmill
collapsed wings
a charred husk
a dead black bird
in the white snow

A Dutch Landscape

The rule of thirds
divides land from sky
a heavy tumble of clouds
over a slip of browns and greens

a small figure
in the foreground
holds a basket
empty or full
I can't know
but they stand
in the lowlands
a sense of some
thin lineage
between us
the broken sky
the golden frame

Homelands

Witten Wieven dwell
in the lowlands
of my grandmother's country
genii locorum of Eefde and Barchem
who burrow in the earthy tumuli
who appear as mists on the grave hills
before generations of women
who gather in mid-winter
exhaling cloud while
dressed in layers of felted wool
holding baskets of bright apples
offerings in exchange
for wisdom or prophecy

Might I ask the same
so far away, here
sick with *nostos*
restless bones
on stolen soil

Might I visit
your grave hills
Witten Wieven
and feel long years
in my fingertips
might that be the thing
that soothes the *-algia*
of estrangement
the mists of your low hills
my basket brims
with pining

GHOSTS

Walk a set ruins
above the Irish Sea
the wind tossing cloud
from the waves into the green
of the Snowdonia mountains

you carry her in your
ephemerous steps
the ghost from the cottage
who wailed soundless
as you woke before dawn

hadn't you seen her
her long hair soaked
her dark mouth a void
spilling impossible grief
as you lay there watching
the sun growing stronger
the shade of her vanishing
with the scream of the gulls

You walk with her now
as you walk with others
their voices are the wind
that batters these stones

INCURSIONS

He's wearing wool
battered leather and his hair
is the grey of the sky
as he points across the Irish Sea
from where you stand
on a Scottish bluff

Mercenaries and murderers
our people left here
and landed there

You nod and feel
this in your boots
you carry their incursions
under your heavy coat

Sour and Rind

Il-mara bhall-lumija taghsarha u tarmiha.
A woman is like a lemon; you squeeze her and throw her away.
                                             —Maltese Proverb

Above the cliffs at Miġra l-Ferħa
where the Mediterranean Sea
batters the ancient island
I walk a narrow path
with my distant relative
who is too thin
fluttering in her pastel dress
she grips my arm
with brittle warmth and whispers
you're lucky you weren't born here

On this island where cruel husbands
find new women in the port towns
the pulsing music and bright lights
beacons for their kind
men who spend
their money there
and leave you poor
in your village
surrounded by the lemon groves
your heart all rind and sour

Maltese Proverbs

In the dark
all women are the same
rise incandescent
their feet quiet serpents
their soft pelts silver
their mouths black iron
they howl knives
and ingest night

Ġgantija

A giantess wakes
salt in her dark hair
stirring in a grove of cypress
outside the village of Ta'cenc
where the brown stonechats chitter
songs from the deserts and sea

When she wakes
the ground venerates
her corpulence
as she feeds herself
broad beans and honey
taking her time
the honey sweet
the eons in her sun-warmed flesh
monoliths in her fingertips

An Old Song

A nude painted in lemon yellow
against a bubble gum pink background
twists from our gaze
her back tall
her knees bent
her hand flat
steadying herself
in his empty space

She's one of hundreds
he paints with gnarled hands
in his studio by sea
where he sometimes
sculpts vulvas or
his own erect phallus
where he fills
rooms with flesh
with nipples pert
in the damp Pacific air
the buttocks rising
like pink–hued mountains
the salt of the sea
and the salt of their skin
coaxing him back
day after day

And I chose her
the lemon yellow woman
when he'd offered me a piece
from his cornucopia of flesh
her body more solid
than most of his nymphs
the folds of her belly
like the folds of my own
her averted gaze
an old song I know

A Giantess

The moon a heavy crescent
over the sleeping valley
over a lake that becomes a river
filled with fish and starlight

In this quiet
she walks soft footed
a giantess stepping gentle
into the valley

Where she walks barefoot
on the empty highway
steps redolent with deep time
she watches

mountains rise jagged
from tilted plates
watches them become
softer hills

watches their continents drift
slow islands under celestial light
she sails

Teeth & Secrets

The lake swallows them
with the taste of salt
three kids on a sandspit
play in the deep fiord
of a lake
that narrows
becomes a river with
a current that cuts
against stone and sand
the green forest still
with the August heat that
settles in the valley basin
the lake's surface
sedate—steady
as they are pulled
through green waters into
dark and more dark
where the lake sturgeon
rest in the icy flows
prehistoric eyes
that see and don't
the small bodies that drift
limp almost elegant
through the depths

At least that's what he tells you
the man in motorcycle leathers
who appears before
the beach blanket
you share with a friend
his white hair a radiance
around his suntanned face
and he leaves you
his boots ponderous
in the too-soft sand
vanishes in the trees
and your friend whispers
that he might have been a ghost
and you nod—agree
look to the lake
hard sparkling
all teeth and secrets

Become the Sea

Languid as a polluted river
I move through detritus
waters viscous
as amniotic fluids
and pour into a gulf
salty as the sea
dark as wine
and warm
I rise like the moon
to devour coastlines
to become the land
to become the sea

Sweater Drawer

In late August when the light that feeds you fades
you pry hot afternoons from the cold mouth of winter
your sweaters and boots wait for your calloused feet
your darkness just there—vapour rising from lakes before dawn

Blue Bird

Mountain blue birds
arrive electric blue
in early April

Surprise us
as we kneel
in freshly thawed soil
our eyes accustomed to
the morning fog
that seals the valley

They gaze quizzically
from naked branches
perhaps pitying us
the winter in our hair
our eyes wide before
their plumage
a forgotten season
in their wings

Manuports

We carry stones
in our pockets
our fingers working
bits of basalt or quartzite

stones that will outlast us
quiet memorials
to our finite migrations

Palimpsests

fly over small blue lakes and grey peaks and go to a city and forget
that place and buy new shoes and furniture and watch days spin
grey into your hair and care less about geography and more about
texts–intertexts–textualities and become pale a palimpsest overwrit-
ten older now with battered lungs and still that soil rests heavy in
your ribcage so go back and dig your way into the mountain
become earth become broken roots become bones that settle here
fly over small blue lakes and grey peaks and go to a city and forget
that place and buy new shoes and furniture and watch days spin
grey into your hair and care less about geography and more about
texts–intertexts–textualities and become pale a palimpsest overwrit-
ten older now with battered lungs and still that soil rests heavy in
your ribcage so go back and dig your way into the mountain
become earth become broken roots become bones that settle here
fly over small blue lakes and grey peaks and go to a city and forget
that place and buy new shoes and furniture and watch days spin
grey into your hair and care less about geography and more about
texts–intertexts–textualities and become pale a palimpsest overwrit-
ten older now with battered lungs and still that soil rests heavy in
your ribcage so go back and dig your way into the mountain
become earth become broken roots become bones that settle here
fly over small blue lakes and grey peaks and go to a city and forget
that place and buy new shoes and furniture and watch days spin
grey into your hair and care less about geography and more about
texts–intertexts–textualities and become pale a palimpsest overwrit-
ten older now with battered lungs and still that soil rests heavy in
your ribcage so go back and dig your way into the mountain
become earth becomes broken roots become bones that settle here
fly over small blue lakes and grey peaks and go to a city and forget
that place and buy new shoes and furniture and watch days spin
grey into your hair and care less about geography and more about
texts–intertexts–textualities and become pale a palimpsest overwrit-
ten older now with battered lungs and still that soil rests heavy in
your ribcage so go back and dig your way into the mountain
become earth becomes broken roots become bones that settle here

Dissolve Here

Sit by the lake at dusk
as the bats rustle
from the silt cliffs
to skim the surface
sit while the snakes
slip over stones
into tepid waters
old and older
languorous now
bats grazing
slow fish in the depths
join then now
in these waters
be this place
dissolve here

Author's Note:

I would like to extend my respect to the First Nations of the West Kootenay and Boundary regions on whose unceded territories I live and work: the Sinixt, the Syilx (Okanagan), and the Ktunaxa.

Parts of this manuscript arose from my doctoral dissertation at York University, where I examined the ongoing settler-colonial making and unmaking of place on unceded Indigenous territories. Through my doctoral research work and in this poetry manuscript, I've returned to British Columbia's southern interior valleys, moving through geographic space and through my own history of trauma, rootlessness and working transiency within its regions.

While the poems in this collection draw on some of my lived experience, they present poetic recollections of experiences over time. Some events have been compressed or are entirely imagined. Any resemblance to actual persons, living or dead, is entirely coincidental.

Earlier versions of some of these poems have appeared in *Event*, *The Puritan*, *Prism International*, *WTF Magazine*, *Prism International*, *Trinity Review*, *Contemporary Verse 2*, *Literary Review of Canada (LRC)*, *The Goose*, *This Magazine*, and *The Antigonish Review*. Many thanks to the editors of each.

Acknowledgements:

I would like to express my sincere gratitude to all those who have played an instrumental role in the completion of this collection.

I am deeply indebted to Leesa Dean for her unwavering friendship, and invaluable editorial guidance, which were crucial in shaping the manuscript. I would also like to extend my heartfelt appreciation to Aaron Tucker for his editorial generosity and words of encouragement that motivated me to bring this book to fruition.

Furthermore, I wish to acknowledge and thank my early writing instructors for their invaluable contributions to my growth as a writer. I am eternally grateful to Almeda Glenn Miller, whose guidance and mentorship during my formative years were instrumental in the trajectory of my writing life. I would also like to thank John Lent, my creative writing instructor at Okanagan College, whose pedagogy and kindness continue to inspire my own teaching practice.

I would also like to thank my mentors and instructors at York University, who encouraged me to go back to the places where I grew up through writing and research. Thank you to Lily Cho, Allan Weiss, Stephen Cain, Len Early, Karen Valihora, for all of your support over the years.

I am also deeply grateful to my support network, including Stephen Rita-Procter, Sarah Jensen, Anna Veprinska, Anna St. Onge, Ruth Ellen St. Onge, Chandra McCann, and Jon Hunter, for their unwavering academic and creative support and encouragement from various corners of the country.

I would also like to thank the remarkable writing community I've found here in the West Kootenays. Thank you to Rayya Liebich and Katie Sawyer (who formed a contingent of our "badass" poetry group). Also thank you everyone at the Elephant Mountain Literary Festival, whose support of the literary arts in this community means so much.

Additionally, I would like to express my appreciation to my colleagues and students at Selkirk College. I feel fortunate to be part of such a vibrant, creative, and supportive community of learners and scholars.

Finally, I would like to thank my husband, Tyler, and my son, Elliot, whose unconditional love, unwavering support, and hilarious pep talks keep me writing. With love and gratitude, I dedicate this collection to you both.

WORKS REFERENCED:

McKay, Don. "Baler Twine: Thoughts on Ravens, Home, and Nature Poetry." *Studies in Canadian Literature / Études en littérature canadienne*, 18.1 (1993): n. pag.

Lane, Patrick. "A Murder of Crows." *The Collected Poems of Patrick Lane*. Eds. Donna Bennett, and Russell Brown. Madeira Park, BC: Harbour Pub., 2011.